THE
MIAMI
DOLPHINS

Published by Creative Education, Inc., 123 South Broad Street, Mankato, Minnesota 56001

Copyright © 1986 by Creative Education, Inc. International copyrights reserved in all countries. No part of this book may be reproduced in any form without written permission from the publisher. Printed in the United States.

Library of Congress Catalog Card No.: 85-72619

ISBN: 0-88682-037-5

THE MIAMI DOLPHINS

JAMES R. ROTHAUS

CREATIVE EDUCATION

PASSING
INTO THE
FUTURE

Danny Marino's eyes dance back and forth, spying the defense. His head jerks up and down as he barks the signals. The center snaps the ball. Immediately, the field is flooded with motion and commotion.

The "Mark Brothers"—wide receivers Mark Clayton and Mark Duper—streak downfield while tailback Tony Nathan circles out of the backfield. Quarterback Dan Marino sees them all. He scans the gridiron patiently even as enemy linemen converge.

Then—in an instant—he strikes. In one blurring motion, Marino plants his right foot, cocks his golden arm and sends a perfect spiral whistling into the waiting arms of Clayton in the end zone. Six points. It should be worth 12!

Ten years ago, most of the kids at Pennsylvania's Central Catholic High School probably would've laughed if you had tried to tell them that the quarterback of their football team would one day become an instant NFL legend with the mighty Miami Dolphins.

"Danny Marino is too scrawny to play pro ball," they would have said. "Besides that, Danny likes to goof around. He'd rather be tinkering with his car or wolfing down a couple of Big-Macs at McDonald's than pushing weights or running windsprints."

Well, Danny isn't scrawny anymore. At 6-foot-3 and 220 well-muscled pounds, the Dolphins' exciting young

Larry Csonka leads interference for Jim Kiick.

quarterback has certainly shown the world that he can hold his own against the giant defensive linemen of the NFL.

If you're a Dolphins fan, you already know how Danny came from the University of Pittsburgh to the Dolphins camp back in 1983 expecting to sit, listen and learn for a couple of seasons. Instead, he was thrust into the starting quarterback role, and he responded by leading the Dolphins to a wild-card playoff berth in his rookie season—and the Super Bowl in his sophomore season!

The entire nation was awestruck at the way the handsome young superstar virtually revolutionized the game with his passing wizardry in 1984. Marino threw more TD passes that year than any other quarterback in pro football history. Week after week, play after play, it was Marino to Clayton. Marino to Duper. Marino to Nat Moore. And for Miami opponents, it was just too much Marino.

"I've heard all that talk about Danny being a goof-off in high school and college," said Dolphin receiver Mark Clayton who also set a new league record in '84 by catching 19 Marino TD passes during the regular season. "But, I don't think people really understand him.

"Danny is the kind of guy who really gets into everything he does," continued Clayton. "Sure, when it's time to fool around, he's the life of the party—the first one to lift everyone's spirits with a good story or a practical joke. But, when it's time to play football, he's all business.

"Danny wants to do his best on every play—that's his secret. He just gets so hyped-up, so pumped-up, because he doesn't want to let the rest of the team down. I'm

Garo Yepremian (1) was a European soccer player before becoming a top kicker.

Wide receiver Paul Warfield makes a successful grab.

that way, too, so we sometimes fight a little. But the Dolphins are still a big, happy football family."

This is the story of that football family. It's the tale of Miami's favorite sons, a team whose history dates back to 1966 when the Dolphins touched the football for the very first time on the very first play of the very first regular-season game of their very first season and immediately ran it all the way for their very first touchdown—a 95-yarder—and never looked back!

FOOTBALL
WITH A
FLIPPER

Danny Marino was only five-years-old when the Dolphins first donned their aqua/coral-colored jerseys for their first season in 1966.

Why were they named the Dolphins? Well, the public demanded it. A few people suggested nicknames such as the Mariners, Marauders, Missiles, Sharks and Suns. But "Dolphins" was by far the most popular entry in a "Name The Team" contest.

"It makes sense," said owner Joe Robbie. "The dolphin is one of the fastest and smartest creatures in the sea. Dolphins can attack and kill a shark or a whale. Sailors say bad luck will come to anyone who harms one of them."

During that first season, the team kept its mascot—a live dolphin named "Flipper"—in a pool at one end of their home stadium, the Orange Bowl. The grinning, bottle-nosed mammal put on quite a show for the fans,

Owner Joe Robbie called Bob Griese the "cornerstone of the franchise." In his 14 seasons at the helm of the Dolphins, Griese was voted All-Pro twice and directed Miami to two straight Super Bowl championships.

which was a good thing, too, because the fans had very little else to cheer.

You see, the Dolphins were born as part of the old American Football League. Miami's first squad was comprised primarily of aging NFL players who could no longer cut it in the "big leagues." Among others, there was Billy Joe, Gene Mingo and a guy named Wahoo McDaniel. Head Coach George Wilson hoped to find some help for them in the college draft.

Miami chose Illinois fullback Jim Grabowski as its No. 1 pick in the '66 draft. Grabowski, who was also drafted by Green Bay of the NFL, wasn't about to play second-fiddle to a dolphin named Flipper; he signed with the Packers. It was the last time the two rival leagues went head-to-head over a college player. Later that year, the AFL and NFL merged to become one united league.

Things did not go well for the Dolphins that first year. They lost their first nine games (four in preseason). The Orange Bowl stood two-thirds empty at most home games. Rookie quarterback Rick Norton broke his jaw at Houston and was lost for the remainder of the season.

Running back Joe Auer was one of the few bright spots for Miami during the 3-11 season. The unheralded free agent scored the club's first-ever touchdown, running back the opening kickoff of the Dolphins' inaugural game 95 yards for a score. He then capped the season by catching a TD pass with 38 seconds left to beat Houston, 29-28.

Over the next three years, Coach Wilson stockpiled lots of talented players. The Dolphins drafted Bob Griese, Larry Csonka, Jim Kiick and Dick Anderson. They traded for Nick Buoniconti, Larry Little and Mercury Morris,

In a rugged playoff game, Bob Griese is mauled by Oakland Raider defensive end Ben Davidson.

then signed a promising free agent named Manny Fernandez. But Miami still failed to pull it all together. The fans were getting tired of watching Flipper; they wanted to watch winning football. Desperate to oblige them, Robbie went looking for a new head coach.

SHULA SHAKES
UP THE
DOLPHINS

In 1970, Robbie found his man, Don Shula. The new Miami coach was one of the youngest mentors in the NFL, yet he boasted a long line of accomplishments. Shula had led the Baltimore Colts to Super Bowl III just a year earlier. When the Colts lost that game to the New York Jets, however, the Baltimore owner had become furious.

Shula was only too glad to leave. The Dolphins would be a fresh start. When he arrived in Miami, Shula said, "I am not a miracle-worker. I have no magic formulas. The only way I know to win is hard work."

The hard-driving Shula put the Dolphins through the wringer in training camp. He helped them expand their talents and exceed their previous expectations. Shula instilled confidence in the young quarterback, Bob Griese. He revived Paul Warfield's career as an outstanding deep receiver. He hired a necktie salesman from Cyprus named Garo Yepremian to be the Dolphins' kicker.

Sure enough, Shula spelled success for the Dolphins. The once-crowded beaches sat empty on Sundays as

Only three teams have ever won back-to-back World Championships: The Green Bay Packers, the Pittsburgh Steelers and, of course, the Miami Dolphins.

In his long career, veteran quarterback Earl Morrall played for the 49ers, the Steelers, the Lions, the Giants, the Colts and the Dolphins. In 1968 he was top passer in the NFL.

Miami fans flocked to see their reborn football team.

A huge throng of 76,712 packed the Orange Bowl to see the Dolphins dump Baltimore, 20-13—and that was only an exhibition game! Miami continued its winning ways in the regular season, opening with four victories in the first five games. But when the team slumped into a three-game losing streak, the fans wanted a new quarterback. Griese ignored their catcalls.

Eventually, Griese settled down and played what Shula called "the perfect game" in a 21-10 triumph over New Orleans. It was the beginning of a six-game victory streak that propelled the young Dolphins into the AFC playoffs for the first time.

In their first post-season contest, Miami met Oakland on a muddy California turf. The Dolphins, behind 14-7, were fighting their way back into contention early in the fourth quarter when everything suddenly went haywire. First, Yepremian missed an easy 24-yard field goal. Then, three plays later, the Raiders scored on a lucky 82-yard bomb from Daryle Lamonica to Rod Sherman. Oakland went on to win, 21-14.

Shula entered the dressing room afterwards wearing neither a smile nor a frown. "Gentlemen, I know you tried your best, and I appreciate your effort," is all he said. Shula was like that.

THE LONGEST GAME

The 1971 season was full of hills and valleys. It saw Bob Griese and Paul Warfield emerge as football's hot-

Miami safety Charles Babb (49) blocks a punt attempt by Cleveland's Don Cockcroft during the 1972 playoff. Babb ran the ball for a touchdown.

test passing combo, while Garo Yepremian became the king of NFL kickers. It also saw Jim Kiick and Larry Csonka land the nicknames "Butch Cassidy and the Sundance Kid" following their outlaw salary holdout. Later, the pair trampled their way to stardom.

It was a year when the Dolphins recovered from a slow start to win eight of their last 10 games to claim the Eastern Division crown with a 10-3-1 record. The highest peak of the season came in the first playoff game, against Kansas City. It was a contest that went down in history as "football's longest day."

The Chiefs, playing at home, built a 10-0 advantage in the first period before Csonka broke one loose for a Miami score. Then, in the dying seconds of the first half, Yepremian knotted the score with a field goal.

The Dolphins battled from behind twice in the second half to tie the game, the last time on Griese's 5-yard TD flip to Marv Fleming with 96 seconds remaining. Still, Miami barely escaped defeat when K.C.'s Jan Stenerud missed a field-goal try from 32 yards with 35 seconds left.

Now, the game went to sudden-death overtime. Stenerud had a 42-yarder blocked by Nick Buoniconti in the fifth period, and Yepremian missed from 45 yards. But early in the second overtime, Csonka rambled 29 yards up the middle, giving Yepremian one more chance to win the game. This time, from 37 yards, Garo's kick sailed straight and true. After 82 minutes and 40 seconds of football, Miami had edged Kansas City, 27-24, in the longest game ever.

Miami went on to rout Baltimore, 21-0, to advance to its first championship game, Super Bowl VI against Dallas.

There has probably never been a better backfield duo than Larry Csonka and Mercury Morris. In 1972, Csonka and Morris became the first NFL backfield to produce two 1,000-yard rushers.

The Most Valuable Player of Super Bowl VII was safetyman Jake Scott (13), shown here as he intercepts a pass intended for Redskin Charley Taylor (42). Scott ran the interception back 55 yards.

Sharp passing by Roger Staubach, slashing running by Duane Thomas and a stout Doomsday Defense paved the way to a convincing 24-3 win by the Cowboys. The Dolphins were heartbroken.

THE PERFECT
SEASON

Don Shula was bitterly disappointed over his club's loss to Dallas. People lauded him as a miracle man for leading the Dolphins into the Super Bowl in just two seasons. But Shula would never be satisfied until Miami was world champion.

There was no doubt that the Dolphins would again be a playoff contender in 1972. But Shula set much higher goals for his team. An unbeaten season was regarded as impossible. Shula disagreed. Anything was possible, he said.

"At the beginning of the season, you don't say to yourself, 'We can't win every football game,'" he explained. "I believe you go out every day trying to win. You set a goal to be the best, and then you work hard every hour of every day, striving to reach that goal. If you allow yourself to settle for anything less than your best, then you are cheating everybody, including yourself."

Before the 1972 season opened, Shula took out some quarterback insurance. He hired veteran Earl Morrall from the Colts as a backup for Griese. In his final year with Baltimore, teammates had teased the 38-year-old Morrall by calling him an "old man" and putting a

NFL Commissioner Pete Rozzelle and owner Joe Robbie congratulate Don Shula, who holds the Vince Lombardi Trophy after leading his players to their second Super Bowl victory in 1974.

Dolphins Vern Den Herder and Kim Bokamper (58) force Raider quarterback Ken Stabler to fumble the ball during the playoff game of 1974.

rocking chair next to his locker. But Morrall would have the last laugh.

When Greise was lost to a broken ankle in Miami's fifth straight victory, Morrall was elevated to first string. His crew-cut hair and conservative style didn't seem to fit into the same backfield with the likes of shaggy Larry Csonka and super-slick Mercury Morris. Yet the threesome melded together to become the most dangerous offensive combination in the NFL.

Morris and Csonka became the first running tandem ever to produce simultaneous 1,000-yard seasons. Csonka, the bullish fullback, packed the pigskin for 1,117 yards while Morris, the lightening-quick speedster, zipped for an even 1,000. Not to be outdone, Morrall led the AFC in passing. Not bad for an "old man."

But here's the best part: They did it without a loss. Miami marched through the season unscathed at 14-0-0. No other team had ever won that many games in a regular season. It was the first "perfecto" since the Chicago Bears had gone 11-0 in 1942.

While Morrall, Morris and Csonka grabbed most of the headlines that season, it was Miami's defense that threw fear into the hearts of enemy offenses throughout the league. They were called the "No Name Defense." There were no famous superstars—just 11 unsung heroes who played flawlessly all year long.

"They don't have any standouts," said Buffalo quarterback, Dennis Shaw. "Their secondary is just four good athletes who work well together. And that's the worst kind of defense to play against because there's nobody you can pick on."

"The nickname doesn't bother us," said Dolphin safety

Steve Towle (56), with a little help from Tim Foley and some other Dolphins, downs a Baltimore ball-carrier.

Speedy Delvin Williams seems to see disaster ahead as he flies down the field.

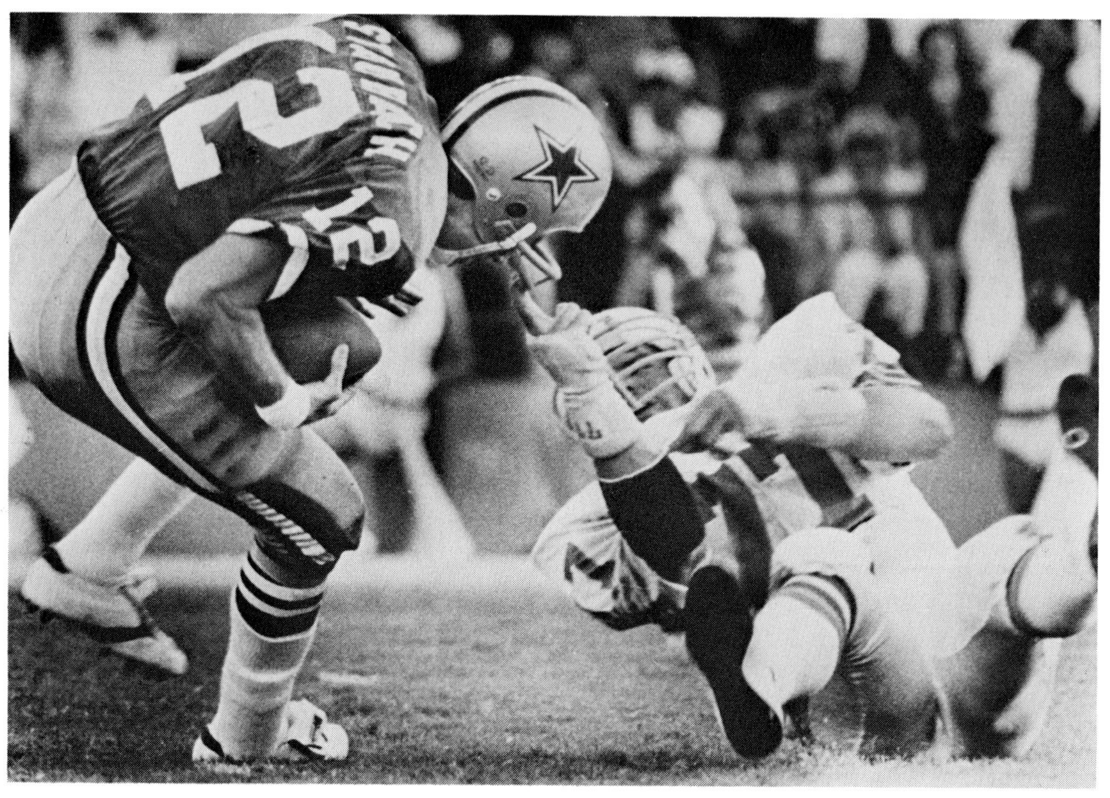

A.J. Duhe seems to be bringing down Dallas quarterback Roger Staubach with a single finger to the face-mask.

man Jake Scott. "I don't care if people remember my name as long as we don't have any losses."

In the opening round of the playoffs, however, Miami came within a whisker of suffering a first and season-ending loss. Cleveland had taken a 14-13 lead with eight minutes to play. But Morrall reached back and rescued the Dolphins, marching them 80 yards for the winning touchdown.

Miami fans grew impatient the next week when Morrall temporarily lost the magic touch against Pittsburgh. The Steelers led the Dolphins, 10-7, in the second half, and Miami was going nowhere. Griese, whose ankle was now mended, nervously paced the sidelines until Shula finally pointed to him. "Get us out of here with a win," the coach barked.

With Griese at the helm, the Dolphins came to life, scoring two touchdowns on runs by Jim Kiick, to win the game, 21-17.

There was only one game left—Super Bowl VII against the Washington Redskins. Miami couldn't risk a slow start against the Skins, so Shula started Griese for the first time in 12 weeks. Griese repaid the favor by unloading a 28-yard touchdown pass to speed merchant Howard Twilley for a quick 7-0 lead.

In the second quarter, Nick Buoniconti emerged from the No Name Defense to steal a Bill Kilmer pass and return it 32 yards, setting up Kiick's 1-yard plunge.

Then, late in the second half, Scott short-circuited an electrifying Washington rally by intercepting Kilmer in the end zone and returning the ball 55 yards. On the Redskins' final drive, with the score 14-7, big Manny Fernandez sacked Kilmer for his 17th tackle. The mighty

The Miami Dolphins have retired Bob Griese's No. 12!

Redskins had been routed. Miami's "impossible dream" had come true. They had gone 17-0-0 and won their first world championship.

"You simply cannot beat this," exclaimed Shula. "This is the ultimate!

"Nobody has ever done what this team has done," the coach reminded. "As far as I'm concerned, this is the finest team I've ever seen." Millions of football fans all over the nation had to agree.

BACK ON TOP

More than any other man, Don Shula admired Vince Lombardi, the late coach of the Green Bay Packers. Both men drove their teams hard, believing that hard work produced championships. Both took losing teams and transformed them into winners. After Super Bowl VII, many people began comparing Shula to Lombardi, and the Dolphins to the great Packer teams of the early Sixties. Green Bay was the only team that had won back-to-back Super Bowls. Could the Dolphins be the next?

"I'd like to think we can do it," said Shula on the eve of the 1973 season. "We would like to write some new history as far as winning is concerned."

Shula didn't get another perfect campaign, but he came close. Miami went 12-2 to win the Eastern Division for the third straight year. Two playoff victories over Cincinnati and Oakland followed. Once again, Miami was in the Super Bowl, becoming the first team to ever get there three consecutive seasons.

Bob Griese, playing in glasses, escapes the thundering Oakland herd.

Buffalo running back Jim Braxton is downed by a pack of Dolphin defenders in a close game played in 1978. Bob Matheson (53) is low man on the totem pole.

The only people standing between them and another championship were the Minnesota Vikings, their scrambling quarterback Fran Tarkenton and a towering defense known as the "Purple People Eaters."

Minnesota was mean. . .but the Dolphins dominated. Griese just shoved the ball into the arms of Larry Csonka and the big bulldozer did the rest. "Zonk," as they called him, battered the Viking line on the opening drive, climaxing the series with a five-yard bolt for a score. Kiick capped the second drive with another TD, and the Dolphins were rolling.

Csonka was running with such authority that Griese seldom had to pass. Csonka put the finishing touches on his day late in the third quarter with another touchdown. He had gained a Super Bowl record 145 yards.

At the end, the score was 24-7; the Dolphins had firmly stamped their names in the history books by winning back-to-back championships.

AN END TO THE
DOLPHIN DYNASTY

In 1974, the two-time defending champion Dolphins went 11-3 and dreamed of a "Triple Crown" when they met Oakland in the semifinal playoff game. Going into the final minutes, Miami led, 19-14. But Kenny "The Snake" Stabler struck with two clutch TD passes to edge out the Dolphins, 28-26.

That loss marked the end of an era. Miami's two-year domination of pro football had come to a close. So had

On January 13, 1974, Larry Csonka bulled his way for a Super Bowl record 145 yards in Miami's 24-7 victory over the Minnesota Vikings for their second World Championship.

On December 12, 1982, the Dolphins suffered a bizarre 3-0 loss in New England. Late in the fourth quarter, a groundskeeper cleared space on the snow-frozen field, enabling the Patriots to kick the winning field goal.

the days of Warfield, Kiick and Csonka. The three offensive stars defected to the ill-fated World Football League.

All Shula could do was patch the holes. Second-year man Benny Malone and veteran Norm Bulaich took turns filling Csonka's shoes. Morris remained at tailback. Nat Moore became Griese's favorite target in place of Warfield. For most teams, a 10-4 record under those conditions would have been termed a success. For the Dolphins, it was the first time in five years that they missed the playoffs.

The Dolphins really took a dive in 1976 when Griese's game fell apart. He complained of blurred vision. Listen to this: Doctors later found that he was legally blind in one eye! If the leader was blind, you can imagine how his followers fared. Miami dropped to just 6-8, giving Shula his first losing season as a head coach.

MIAMI MARCHES ON

While Shula needed to completely rebuild the defense in 1977, the offense didn't change much. Oh, there was a new look for Bob Griese. The Dolphin quarterback now wore heavy black eyeglasses.

But if ever a pro quarterback was meant to wear eyeglasses, it was Bob Griese. He was barely 6-1 and had the biceps of a librarian. Griese looked more like a frail, studious chess-master than an NFL quarterback.

Looks aren't important; actions are. Sporting his new glasses in 1977, Griese saw his way through his finest year as a pro, throwing 22 touchdown passes. His most memorable performance came in a 55-14 rout of St.

Garo Yepremian tries for a field goal while reserve quarterback Don Strock holds the ball.

Oiler Earl Campbell comes out on top of the heap, scoring in the 1978 playoff game and spoiling Dolphin hopes for that year.

Louis when he threw six scoring passes, one short of the NFL record. Twelve of Griese's TD strikes went to Nat Moore, who had come on to become the league's best deep-threat.

The Dolphins' new-found offense combined with a young, aggressive defense (spearheaded by rookies A.J. Duhe and Bob Baumhower) to earn Miami a share of the Eastern Division crown with a 10-4 record. Because of a complicated tie-breaker formula, however, the Baltimore Colts claimed the division's only playoff spot.

In 1978, Miami suffered a similar fate, again losing the division title on a tiebreaker. This time, however, they did qualify as a "Wild Card" playoff entry. The Dolphins' 1-2 backfield punch of Leroy Harris and Delvin Williams (who had gained a team record 1,258 yards during the regular season) was held to only 84 combined yards in the 17-9 loss to Houston.

The next season, Dolphin defenders decided to take matters into their own hands. The supercharged Miami stop-squad held opponents to less than two touchdowns in nine games during 1979. That was also the year that Larry Csonka returned to the club after a four-year absence. His bullish running, combined with Griese's pinpoint passing, paved the way to a 10-6 mark and an outright division championship.

A quarterback controversy marred much of the 1980 campaign as Griese sat on the bench while younger understudies David Woodley and Don Strock fought for the No. 1 job. Sadly, it marked the end of Griese's 14-year career as the Dolphins' "thinking man's quarterback." He never set any league records in that time, but he did win over 100 games for Miami. "And the bottom line," said Griese, "is winning. That's all that interested me."

STAR SEARCH

Woodley emerged as the starting QB in 1982, and he did a heckuva job, too. Thanks to Woodley's quiet, steady leadership, the Dolphins went back to the Super Bowl with a 7-2 record in that strike-shortened season.

An eighth-round draft choice out of Louisiana State, Woodley had barely made the cut. Now, just two years later at the age of 24, here he was—the youngest starting quarterback in Super Bowl history. Would the older, more experienced Redskins head him off at the pass? Here's what happened:

Woodley's gorgeous 76-yard scoring pass to a streaking Jimmy Cefalo gave Miami a 7-0 lead, but that woke the Redskins up. It took a field goal by Uwe von Schamann and a scorching 98-yard kickoff return by Fulton Walker to keep Miami in the game, 17-10, with 10 minutes left.

It was then that the Redskins placed their faith in John Riggins, their big, burly running back. The Miami defense was tired, but Riggins just seemed to run harder and harder with each carry. With "Big John" leading the way, Washington scored 17 points in those final minutes, six points coming on a 43-yard burst by Riggins, to win the 1982 World Championship, 27-17.

Though the Dolphins had fallen one game short of a world title, Woodley still appeared to be everyone's

Reggie Roby, one of the greatest punters in NCAA history, was a welcome addition to the Dolphins in 1983.

NBC
Sport

choice for Miami quarterback of the future. Still, when Pittsburgh's Dan Marino became available in the 1983 college draft, Shula did not hesitate to take him. "Give Marino four or five years and he might be a starter," the scouts advised Shula.

Marino, who had struggled through a lackluster senior season in college, began his pro career as the Number 3 QB behind Woodley and Strock. His strong arm and poise in the pocket impressed the coaches, but they still felt he needed seasoning.

A few weeks into the '83 campaign, however, Strock was sidelined with a foot injury so Marino moved up to No. 2. Up until Game 5, Marino never saw any game action. But when Woodley failed to move the Miami offense against New Orleans, Shula called on Danny. "See what you can do," said the coach.

Marino had a case of the butterflies. He started off by tossing a shaky pass that was quickly intercepted for a Saints touchdown. That did it. Now, Marino's great competitive drive rose up within him. As the game wore on, his confidence grew stronger and stronger. The rest of the Miami offense responded. Late in the game, they drove into New Orleans territory and Danny hurled a rocket to Mark "Super" Duper for a touchdown. Though Miami would lose that game to the Saints, they would go on to win the war.

Shula had seen enough. "I like the spark Marino gives to our offense," he told the press. With the Dolphins' record at 3-2, Shula decreed that Marino would get the starting nod the following week against Buffalo. Danny threw three touchdowns against the Bills, and the rest is history.

Before 1984, no Miami quarterback had ever passed for more than 3,000 yards. That season, Dan Marino shattered team and league passing marks by throwing for an incredible 5084 yards and 48 TD's!

Danny and the Dolphins went on to win nine of their last 11 games to sew up the 1983 Eastern Division crown. Marino's statistics included 20 TD passes in nine starts. He was voted Rookie of the Year and AFC Offensive Player of the Year for his efforts. What's more, he had proved all the experts wrong by contributing big numbers immediately, not after four or five years. Miami's star search was over; the Dolphins had found their man.

MARINO SCORES WITH PASSING MARKS

Marino really came into his own in 1984…and so did the rest of the Dolphins. No record was safe from them.

The old Miami record for yards passing in a game was 408 set by Woodley. Marino beat that with 429 yards against St. Louis in Week 5. He then raised the standard to 470 against the Raiders later in the season.

It took Marino only eight games to break Bob Griese's season yardage record of 2,473. By the end of the campaign, Marino had shattered the NFL mark with 5,084 yards and—here's one for Ripley's Believe It Or Not—48 touchdown passes!

The Dolphins' final scores resembled basketball totals. Never did they score less than three TD's in a game. Club and league records toppled every week as Miami marched methodically toward another Super Bowl.

"Marino is the closest thing I've ever seen to being unstoppable," said head coach Mike Ditka of the Chicago Bears—and Ditka is not one to hand out compliments.

Big Doug Betters had a truly sensational season in 1983-84. His top honor was being named NFL's Defensive Player of the Year by AP.

"Our offensive philosophy is just three words: Go for it!" said Shula. "I don't even tell Danny what to do. He just goes out there and throws. When he's on, and he usually is, there's not much anyone can do about it."

Of course, Marino had plenty of help. All-Star receivers Mark Duper and Mark Clayton were rated as the best in the NFL at their positions. Clayton caught 19 TD passes from Marino—another NFL record. Running backs Tony Nathan and Woody Bennett combined for over 1,000 yards.

On defense, the "Killer B's" came out swarming, especially at the end of the regular season and playoffs. In all, Miami's "B-fense" featured nine players whose last name began with B. They were Doug Betters, Bob Baumhower, Kim Bokamper, Bob Brudzinski, Jay Brophy, Mark Brown, Charles Bowser, and the "Brothers Blackwood," Lyle and Glenn.

Needless to say, Miami was the class of the AFC Eastern Division in 1984 with a 14-2 record. Few teams could keep pace with the Dolphins' prolific passing attack for more than a quarter. Their playoff opponents were no exception. Miami shot down the Seattle Seahawks, 31-10, and the Pittsburgh Steelers, 45-28.

The only team capable of outscoring the Dolphins was their Super Bowl XIX opponents, the San Francisco 49ers. If anyone could keep up with Marino, it was Joe Montana of the 49ers.

In the final two weeks leading up to the big game, sportswriters argued about who was the game's best quarterback, Marino or Montana. In the end, they agreed that whoever won the Super Bowl would get the unofficial title of best QB in the land.

Here's the one-and-only Mark "Super" Duper in action (1984).

As of 1985, the Miami Dolphins had played in nine overtime games, more than any other NFL club.

Marino looked like he had the edge early, connecting with tight-end Dan Johnson for a touchdown late in the first quarter to give Miami a 10-7 lead. After that, however, it was all Joe Montana.

Calmly, Joe led the Niners to three unanswered touchdowns. That pretty much put the game out of reach—even for the high-scoring Dolphins. Marino simply could not get untracked, and Miami stalled. With the "Killer B's" unable to stop Montana, San Francisco rolled to a 38-16 lead before Joe left the game.

Shula couldn't hide his disappointment in the locker room. For the longest time, he didn't say anything. Finally, he spoke.

"It was strange," he said. "Our offense had been slowed down this season, but today was the first time we had been stopped.

"Still, I'm proud of this team," he added. "I hope it will be said that this team showed class and dignity both in victory and defeat." Indeed.

WATCH OUT, NFL!

You can't keep the Dolphins and their fans down for long. During the summer of 1985, Shula, Marino and Co. were busy making plans for their comeback.

The fans? Even during the off-season, enthusiastic members of the Dan Marino fan club walked the streets of Miami in bright, red "Marino Corps" T-shirts, and the city's sportwriters were still churning out daily stories with headlines like, "What's Danny Boy Up To, Now?"

Well, he wasn't goofing off, that's for sure. Even dur-

Mark Clayton exploded for a new club record in punt return yardage in '83.

ing the off-season, Danny had volunteered to spend three days a week, five hours a day, working on special drills at the Dolphins' training camp. He didn't have to do this, he wanted to.

"I want to be the best quarterback in the NFL," he explained. "One great season doesn't make you the best. You've got to be ready to go out there and do it, year after year. That's what guys like Blanda, Namath, Griese and Fouts did, and I want to earn the right for my name to be mentioned with theirs."

Coach Don Shula likes that kind of talk. So do Mark Clayton, Mark Duper and the entire "Killer B's" defense. As a matter of fact, just about everyone in the city of Miami and the state of Florida likes to hear that kind of talk. The only folks who don't are those who live in other NFL cities throughout the land.

Before long, the Miami Dolphins could be the only team in pro football to own their own stadium. The club is planning to build a new 73,000-seat stadium in north Dade County before 1987.

Danny Marino asked for a new contract for 1985, and he got one that matched his on-field statistics. Big!